D1024283

Exceptions and Melancholies

For Phyllis,

for all your kinds
of music (on the page
and in your dancing),
and in friendship,
always, *[signature]*

Montpelier
Jan. 2007

Exceptions and Melancholies
Poems 1986–2006

Ralph Angel

Sarabande S▨ Books

LOUISVILLE, KENTUCKY

FIRST EDITION

Library of Congress Cataloging-in-Publication Data

Angel, Ralph, 1951–
  Exceptions and melancholies : poems, 1986-2006 / by Ralph Angel.—1st ed.
      p.   cm.
  ISBN 1-932511-41-5 (hardcover : alk. paper) — ISBN 1-932511-42-3 (pbk. : alk. paper)
  I. Title.
  PS3551.N457E93 2006
  811'.54—dc22   2006006806

ISBN-13: 978-1-932511-41-3 (cloth)
ISBN-13: 978-1-932511-42-0 (paper)

Cover image: *Untitled* by Sue Williams, provided courtesy of the artist

Manufactured in Canada
This book is printed on acid-free paper.

Sarabande Books is a nonprofit literary organization.

THE KENTUCKY ARTS COUNCIL

The Kentucky Arts Council, a state agency in the Commerce Cabinet, provides operational support funding for Sarabande Books with state tax dollars and federal funding from the National Endowment for the Arts, which believes that a great nation deserves great art.

I fall into melancholies of honey and roses which are none the less melancholy. . . . I assure you that there is only one pleasure: learning what one does not know, and one happiness: loving the exceptions.

—George Sand

CONTENTS

from *Anxious Latitudes*

from *Neither World*

from *Twice Removed*

ACKNOWLEDGMENTS

The following sections of this volume were previously published as books:

Anxious Latitudes. Copyright © 1986 by Ralph Angel, published by Wesleyan New Poets.

Neither World. Copyright © 1995 by Ralph Angel, published by Miami University Press, Oxford.

Twice Removed. Copyright © 2001 by Ralph Angel, published by Sarabande Books, Inc.

Grateful acknowledgment is made to the following periodicals in which the poems in *Exceptions and Melancholies* first appeared: *The American Poetry Review, The American Voice, The Antioch Review, Cimarron Review, College English, Colorado Review, Crazyhorse, Denver Quarterly, Faultline, Hayden's Ferry Review, McSweeney's, The Missouri Review, New Orleans Review, The New Review of Literature, The New Yorker, Partisan Review, Passages North, Ploughshares, Poetry, Pool, Quarry West, Runes, The Southern Review, Third Coast, TriQuarterly, Volt, William & Mary Review.*

Also to the following anthologies: *Anthology of Magazine Verse & Yearbook of American Poetry, The Best American Poetry, The Body Electric, Forgotten Language, The Gertrude Stein Awards in Innovative Poetry, Manthology, Poets of the New Century, The Grand Passion, New American Poets, The Pushcart Prize XIX, Under the Rock Umbrella.*

"Vertigo" is for Alfred Hitchcock; "Part I: Acknowledgment" is for John Coltrane; "a picture of it" is for de Kooning; "Decalogue" is for Krzyztof Kieslowski; "Interior Landscape" is for Helen Frankenthaler.

Exceptions and Melancholies

New Poems

With Care

Whoever has a quiet mind

up on the roof the season turned the bath towels purple.

Quiet is the demolition. The neighbors got to know each other
someday soon.

Boys pull apples to the ground. Clouds
keep the sky together. And the hardest-working part of it steps
        from window scenes

into a pair of jeans, wouldn't you?

I said I found lakes there
and odd pieces of meaning that have nothing to do with you

and wink back. A loon for the first time

sounds like a loon.
Yip yip coyote. I said above the gas station

next door to the animal hospital

know what I mean? Quiet
the bobcat descending the stairs. A racoon

looks in on you when he's away. In our white and blue city
everything smells like a story.

The Unveiling

As it is it could be
fog upon the eve of your unveiling,
or memory—unspooling every
distance—
or the mockingbird,
or the muffled screams of a neighbor,
or laughter—from strangers come
relatives and friends,
and small bowls of vinegar
in a roomful of thinking about you,
the almonds, the prayers
and the figs.

Impossible,
like the unwashed letters of your name,
or the faintly wailing
sirens of childhood, or the ocean
a half mile away—
like a kiss on the cheek,
a flutter of trees
in the plaza,
the breath of every
person you'll be.

Skittering

There is no staying here
except we who are set apart and different
observe ourselves and say "Thank you, a coffee,
yes, and toast, too."
This *is* tomorrow. Scissors
and silverware, a pencil on the table,
we have to keep escaping
always into something like a courtyard
where the salt breeze trembles with branches
and nothing has changed
for decades. No one is lost again
on the surface of the pool.

Then all of a sudden
I am as much as sitting at the desk
of a man bewildered by my being here
and by the clouds behind me
skittering across
the skyline, and maybe
somewhat shaken, too, it's hard to say,
what with loneliness and
everything alive inside
fitting easily
into its metal frame.

You are the perfect distance
when I think of you
I can't see down the road too far, thank God,

not all the time.
This late in the season
the promenade is nearly deserted,
its few words wandering aimlessly
here and there in the quiet
occurring just now.
Pigeons have battered
senseless the archways and the highest doors,
but my heart is not complaining.
That's why, but never mind,

what I'm trying to say
makes faint scratching sounds
upon the paper,
and if the message is less than clear, tonight,
my love, please know
that I'm just a little
out of practice.

Vertigo

Only one is a wanderer.
And when she was sad she'd go into the street to be with people.
Two together are always going somewhere. They lie down beneath
        cypress,
next to a bird. I imagine the sky. It fans her mountains
and waves. She'd left some small town
where they used to make tires.
Stories are made out of stairwells
and rope. I'd been interrupting for years and didn't
know it. This old park. The dark hatchery. Workers in jumpsuits
throw down their poison at dawn.
Not everyone can be described. It's perfectly
natural. If she's thinking about love
does she break down

the door of the bedroom. Of course not. Not publicly
speaking. To the left there's a sofa. We all lived in rented rooms.
That's how it goes with subject matter.
Nude figures in profile
floating among palm trees. The idea was touristy,
like a postcard. I was given a small auditorium. I watched over
rush hour. I write down everything as I forget it,
especially at night.
I lock the door from the inside.

Nobody's Dead There

The road sloped
mostly sideways. It's okay
that I'm sleepy. The moon on the lake
followed us home.
Today's rain is more tropical. No family
anywhere, or that sense
of cold.

It's important not to
yell at your neighbor. It's what she
wants you to do. I only hate
what I pity. I am a transitory and not too disgruntled
citizen of a city deemed
sleepless
for the sake of its very small
fishes. You are
my tongue.

We must attend to
and bless the amenities. We wash our hands
and go nuts. I know morning's
crazy. I know
bread.
A few slices were once
used as stepping stones. Thank God
for friends. I hear the thrush

repeating itself.
There's a prayer for that
too, remember?
We eat less and less. We run and we
exercise. The whole point is to open old wounds and
not talk.
Only then is the quiet
nothing more than the sound of the tires.
To this day, knock
on wood.

First Impressions

Like a ghost

one learns to say no
there's room enough I assure you

It's how a car rolls into a pepper tree

She chews on the straps
of her purse

It's how we arrive in a certain house
at a given time

in the glen

It isn't language that keeps leaving

I ink in the tulips

Here's the white wall of heaven
and the heart that

walks beside me like feeling

The Heart of Things

And so say nothing of the birds
out back, or how the leaves of trees grow louder
than the city, how a room
begins again as though it had been taken away
only. Whatever now
that I'm afraid of, but casually, like someone
sitting crosswise in her chair, her legs
curved over one side, sipping a glass of wine
and spying on her neighbors,
not ill-arranged things really, but that sense
of realism that takes up a lot more time
than I or anyone together
has to give.

And so stayed longer, he said, into the evening
behind the page and out of the cold,
even the dead are free again
to love us as in life a human being
is singled out and standing there, on the curb,
shifting the way we do from
foot to shoeless foot,

and so broke
apart the vision I expected
of myself, confused among those
dozing on the platform, and at home the air
is moist again with tea, but
faintly so, those fragrant several moments

that sound the most like dream,
like dreaming aloud the nightmare
that I alone am still.

Exceptions and Melancholies

Never before
had we been so thin and so clear
and arranged always
and in the same way gazing and listening
over the rooftops
to tin cans of flowers and strange
music. For an hour or more
I turned the same corner
and felt like a criminal farther and farther out to sea
among the racks of shoes and old clothes
but now looking
back I should never have
unpacked. A street
crowned with chestnut trees
ends at the sewer. You go to a theatre
and find yourself a house
outside the city
and walk the shore
forever. I don't have much
talent for poetry. When I see a wrecking ball
dangling from a crane I mean it
literally. I mean
I don't mean the world's fallen apart
or that a wrecking ball
symbolizes the eye my world-weary sister
couldn't know to turn away
from. The hospital's

exhausted. The little church is boarded up.
We leaned against the limestone
and liked the fact that tea
sweetens gradually
and that the wildflowers
beneath the shade of trees gone shivering
have really livened up the cemetery
and that the tall grass and the garbage
and especially the piled-up
newspapers and the rooftop pool
fit right in among
these windowless buildings
having gathered
as we are in the flesh again
and leading another life
altogether.

Respite

By then the evening light came in low
to greet us. A fine rain hung suspended in the air.
Maybe you had already begun to want to die.
You took me by the arm, or we held hands. We went to see
a movie, or window shopped, or ate somewhere.
So many impossible things have happened
I am not surprised that we are sitting
reading in the living room. Pine wood crackles
in the fireplace, and when I look up
your eyes are closed, and with your free hand
play piano on my knee. And later,
though the night is young, you kiss my
forehead and smooth my cheeks, whispering
"Let's leave the dishes, darling,
and crawl into bed."

Inside Out

Outside the summer heat was shimmering
and after resting on the beach
I walked until the bay
grew saucer-shaped again
and blue, and so the bowl of pears and even the binoculars
were painted there, and from every
room pushed the land
away.
The light never stopped returning
to the turrets and the cornices above the frieze
above the blondest dog
I'd ever seen,
and public
prayer
was private, a kind of private music
in which a dog might
nose around.

I hate you more than ever
for thinking you don't matter. I am making you
a painting inside my heart a dream
cooks a meal and
oversleeps
again. The mice say "hi"
and crazy starving birds tumble

down the leaves.
Two loves
at least, I imagine three.
No I don't. Hate's the wrong word, too.

Part I: Acknowledgment

We spin
and we deny it.
We speed through space and
hold our ground. We stand firm.
We sprawl out
in the shadows of cobwebs
and swim to the surface
and toast again the staggering
stars and the planets
and our getting away from it all.
We're nobody's business—
and the truth,
the truth's wooden-clock voice
actually lives here.

When the night sky
for example is spattered with paint
and the forest is reduced
to a few glowing windows
and a curlicue of smoke
above a train,
I was at once inside
our cabin afterall, and frankly
sick of friends, though
not the close ones,
of people, maybe,
not you.

Like something in the body
reflecting streets and chance interiors
and yelling Silence,
Camera,
your heart, your
family, inappropriately,
your clothes
against my idiocy,
not you.

Soft and Pretty

You don't even know how old
and black my blood is
or how the world does not participate
though in this country once the elevator's working
and the birds are fed and now they're bathing
and like a train
with a broken arm and blown-out
veins and one good eye you know my story
still, and so sit beside the mind that loses
as it wins you know
in its heart and peel an orange
against the shoulder of a friend and somewhere
clean to sleep
and bring back knowledge of the parapet
so to speak above the sea
and die for slippers and a robe
and in death
drag like waves your sound.

Blackouts

rolled through the city.
Whoever has an answer won't last.
Traffic muscles through. Whole families lazing on steps
eating grapes. "No I'm not," says the youngest
to her canary. "You grew into your legs,
Tall One, didn't you." Then
no one. Loosed papers
flatten the fences. Bits of glass rest there
and burn. This part of nature
runs along ridges, sprouts
wings in the valleys and wanders
the world like a candle. A general steps
down from his pedestal. Everyone
hated that statue. She points
left and says "right." She could be
an orchid. All those seen from afar moving away
from the market. This part of nature
breaks down the butterfly, this part of man
into flutes. Flop
through your branches,
naked one. In room after room, your
strangers have raised you.

The Coast

1.

A necklace of fire
in the foothills. A papery light, at night,
in traffic. You could paint with it. Alongside
a warehouse a palm tree
flares.

Another
hillside is about to open. At the edge
of death the earth
turns. A child
dances,

the wind
goes singing by.

2.

We are traveling to the coast for the weekend. And as on
some stroll through the dusk

the kelp and the cliffs rough up the moon, the tide's
no more lost or pure than being here.

Chandeliers prefer us—
we dine alone.

3.

We are propping up
the bougainvillea. We're planting
iceberg rose. The rains are near, we don't much
suffer, the stones themselves
are wrong.

Like ice
just floating there,
the pain of a toothache, and the plum and the black
bamboo. You could be
the center. Even my mouth, at night,

assaulted by the sirens
and our quarreling, blooms against
your back.

Untitled

for Betty Ong

Something stayed in the mind there.
The most credulous birds. An indifferent
road.
    That
that future is ashes
and a kiss on the cheek. This cup
of coffee goes down like chocolate. A footbridge
the eye leaves among cliff sides
of steam.

    There is no shame
in failure. No lost
or blue unfurling courtyard. You are transparent,
in the basement,
        by way of all exits.

Playing Monster

Of sprinklers
on the tilted lawns, a child,

the lions of repose smoothly sculpted
from the first steps
of a civilized but unrelenting
privacy,

the babble of the run-off.

When I'm in doubt
I am the sound that separates itself
from a leaf-blower
that comes inside with its flock
of parrots.

I think my body's breaking down

where a good friend isn't
actually.

I don't smoke for years,
I don't keep spirits, when I'm insane I close
my eyes and immerse myself

in a warm bath

where the afternoon sun

goes around
behind the house and my sisters
enter boldly. Our voices are all mixed up—
"Here, have another piece of cake." "Let me see
your tongue." "Who
poo'd?"—

we're jumping up and down
and shrieking, we're
running from the willow to the fig tree,
we're hiding
behind the swing set,

and suddenly Vicki's
crying, and so Joanne is crying, too,
all three of us crying and huddled together

as I am now my dear brave
sisters, finally.

Phosphorescence

Only when I looked away did I wear
a woolen cap and winter coat to confuse myself
and give in to the rot and the decay
of months and days of rain and mud seeping
through the windows,
and didn't I dream as always
the most northern
of the islands and of their
phosphorescence,
and wasn't it the one cold day
I could not remember that threw me
from behind the bar repeated sideways glances
and though the news was sad
I just had to laugh, having
read the book.

Even when the sidewalks
are spread with sunglasses and a woman
with a hat steps away from her
reflection and takes
her pulse, and I notice for the first time
the tables in the alley and the unsafe
distance between the tracks
and the brittle walls
I walked down
when nothing came to me
but time,

don't I love dusting off the crumbs
and drinking lukewarm coffee
as a woman with a cane
tells me that her husband was a fisherman
before she outlived him, and though I can't
understand a word she's saying, that her daughter
in her middle age has met a man
who wears too much jewelry
but loves her back,
and who wouldn't help her to her feet
and count her tiny steps
and walk her to the restaurant
above the seawall

that her nephew owns, she tells me,
with its thick aroma of garlic
and roasted peppers,
where she can watch the small boats drift in,
one by one, and that after
dark swells with
dancing and traditional
music.

Steamed Fish and Vegetables

It's a beautiful thing to break open
a cookie and read "You are worried about
something that will never happen"
since only a cookie like that
could get me worrying
about things I never even
dreamed of worrying about
and then stop.

Big tips for everyone!

I was alone, of course,
disheveled from the long flight,
exhausted, really. And grateful, therefore,
for the attentive waiters. But why three cookies?
"Triplets!" cries the next one
as if that might explain it.
Great news, I say,
and mean it.

I shake each waiter's hand.
I thank the chef profusely for her steamed
fish and vegetables. They smile
broadly, but they could tell,
not the truth of it, but
something.

I walk the long half-block
back to my hotel. I felt dejected,
totally spent. But what do I care, I think,
stepping into the elevator.
It's a cookie!

Sampling

I'm standing still on 10th Street. I'm not the only one.
        Buildings rise like foliage and human touch.

And so shall dig this cigarette as my last, and rattle trains, and
        rot the fences of the gardens of my body—

or without the harmony of speaking here the many sounds
        and rhythms that sound a lot like anger

when anger's silent, like a painting, though in the stillness of the
        paint itself the painter nods or waves or asks for help.

I'm not the only one. The pharmacy's untitled. The stars are
        there at night. In this humidity

the forlorn singing of the insects clings to anything nailed
        down. A whole bag of things I'm working

through, some set things that I know, like words I know that
        mean "from one place to another," the word that means

"to carry." I'm standing still on 10th Street. I'm not the only
        one. The dark tastes of salt and oranges. Its eyes

wander round and round. I am its thousand windows. I think
        about the future and the sea. And stay.

Who Knew

Or as I'm shaving here my face again
and throat, I stand before you as myself alone as I can be—go
         figure—the steam! the steam!

Last night I dreamed again from one eye
total blindness—a riverbank of stumbling kittens—a first
family of ducks—in the mirror of my exposure, I admit it, the
         view's enough!
Enough already!—

I walk above the evening. I approach the dark and pull away. I
         move alongside an old dog's
steaming coat—You could have told me all about that. I
         could've
said a lot of things. Who knew!—

If this were my apartment
the dusk opens up its arms again, and so the swallows
cast about. The hills collapse. Every human voice, collectively, is
         murmuring and near.
It's good. It's nice—
who knew!

There'd be more chairs and pillows, and sprouting
herbs and fucked-up wiring—I'm not forgetting anything
         outside my fear that I would find my body
by myself, alone—it's what it's good for—

and set my mind
down on the ground again—
and not remember. Any old life, after all, could be improved upon—
that I'd remain in a cold place.

Brighten

The groves brighten the hillsides,
and further out the pale ribbon of the sea.
It was still dark.
The uneven road carried me along
as surely as my own footsteps.
I had my shoes in my hand.
My knees felt good.
I had my harmonica.

I swam further out then,
away from the songbirds and the laughing
banana trees, and the small wooden
houses painted in lunatic colors.
When I was the blues
I was listening.

Soon the last reveler
dances alone in the fountain.
Soon the market overflows with flowers
and headless octopi.
I'm already singing a station
that takes hours to get to.
I'm complaining for the sake of tobacco.
I'm wailing over the tiled passages
and the endless plunge
of the stairs.

I love the sound of the waves
bumping the sides of the fishing boats.
I love the echoing heart
of the water.
I listen to the soot
and the chatter of dishes.
I listen to faces.
Soon the small beach is noisy
with tourists.
I have my harmonica.
I'm singing for the passengers

coming toward me
and for those behind glass.
When I'm the blues I keep swimming.
I'm singing
for my own stupid luggage.

Sometimes an Image

A long time ago
I dug their graves with sticks. I leaned my face
upon them.

I'm looking at the moon
from our new home on the second floor. From our balcony
of weeds the moon's at sea. It will never snow here

and when it snows the further that I rise
above the earth the better.
I take a hundred

photographs. I
sleep among our clothes.

I don't know if I spoke aloud or not. I don't
stop talking. A long time ago the sky
invented flesh

and the miracle of viewing from a certain
distance the goddess

I need as much as water.

a picture of it

And when you're
through another dream
takes a walk among the ferns
and fragments.
Your garden runs
away.
It is a streaming
fountain—a breeze that
makes of
time the many passing
branches, a broken
tile
of nothing in your way.
As if you
nudged a narrow
shoal of sand
upon the currents
of the sky, and propped
against the whitewash
bougainvillea and
glare.
A lizard
flits across the flagstone,
and then a shadow
filled with birds—
all pink heat
and someone sitting there.

from *Anxious Latitudes*

History

The engines' eternal rumbling. I never get used to it.
Night smoke. Steel dust. The sickly
sawww and *sskreee* of wheels holding the rail.

Never get used to rigid awake, throatful
of ashes and oil. Tons of knuckle. Tons of tightening
slack. Of erosion, impact, tons of freight car.

Never the yard light, wax of formaldehyde.
Never the switch list in the eye's spittle.
Never a charred nerve

that drifts from the cold forest of thinking.
Thinking that a man's five impossible senses
can be that far away.

2

A night wears on, but grows no older.
And a man, a man lights a cigarette
and walks on dirt and thinks he is building

a train. We know the task so well that
knowledge is a blindfold, and for every
thrown switch and passed signal,

for each load of lumber and coal, fuselage
and tank, the routine proceeds no further
than loneliness. So many hours

after school, gathering flat stones and pieces of
dull glass, sending them skipping over
dusk on the lake. The mute chorus

of tree bark and twigs, feathers, the twitching
reeds in the shore water. It's not just the renewal
but the way these mounds of spilled

wheat and sugar, etched with rat tracks, are drawn
into the strange mutterings of men walking toward death.
A single, empty cattle car on the bend—

the smell of shit and straw, the horribly
normal expressions of human beings
reduced to animal heart and animal bone

because there's a history too large,
because there are men who think they write the story.
And we go on interrupting a life that's out of our hands.

A man bashes a 2-x-4 to splinters on the side of a boxcar.
He lines up pennies on the track so that the wheels might
smear them into something new.

3

Slowly methodically,
clanking and bumping over the switches,
a long drag is pulled out toward the main.

Forty, maybe sixty cars,
and the last unfolds the whole of the north end.
Out of emptiness, a cat's squeal

and the cat scrambling across the tracks.
A newspaper lifts up, and touches back.
Shreds of cloth on a broken post.

A moth, dizzy and circling.
And an old guy, coughing, stumbling out of some bushes.
He watches an owl scissor past the tower.

He looks down to twisted cable and busted cans,
to a crumpled shoe as pale as dirt.
He shoves his hand in his pocket, and looks over at me.

You Are the Place You Cannot Move

You wake up healthy
but you don't feel right. Now everything's
backwards and you're thinking of someone to blame.

And you do, you're lucky,
drinking coffee was easy, the traffic's
moving along, you're like
everyone else just trying to get through the day
and the place you're dreaming of seems possible—
somewhere to get to.

All you really know
is that it hurts here, the way feelings
are bigger than we are, and a woman's face
in a third-story window, her limp hair
and pots of red geraniums luring you
into her suffering until you're walking on roads
inscribed in your own body. The maps
you never speak of. Intersections, train stations,
roadside benches, the names of places and
people you've known all bearing the weight
of cashing a check or your heaving to eat something,
of glimpsing the newspaper's ghoulish headlines.

Like everyone else, you think,
the struggle is toward a better time, though
no pressure surrounds the house you were born in.
Cool, quieter, a vast primitive light

where nothing happens but the sound
of your sole self breathing.
And you've decisions to make—isn't that why
you've come?—with a baldheaded man at the bar
and your friends all over the place, anxious,
tired, a little less sturdy than you'd hoped for
and needing someone to kick around, someone to love.

Man in a Window

I don't know   man   trust is a precious thing
a kind of humility   Offer it to a snake and get repaid with
        humiliation

Luckily   friends rally to my spiritual defense
I think they're reminding me

I mean it's important to me   it's
important to me   so I leave my fate to fate and come back
I come back home   We need so much less   always   always
and what's important is always ours

I mean I want to dedicate my life to those who keep going just
        to see how it isn't ending

I don't know
Another average day
Got up putzed around 'til noon
took a shower and second-guessed myself   and
all those people   all those people passing through my
my days and nights   and all those people   and
and you just can't stay with it   you know what I mean
You can't· can't   stay with it   Things happen
Things happen   Doubt sets in   Doubt sets in   and
I took a shower about noon   you know   and I shaved and
thought about not shaving but I
shaved   I took a shower and had a lot of work to do but I

I didn't want to do it   I was second-guessing myself   that's
        when doubt got involved

I struck up a
rapport with doubt   I didn't do any work   and so
and so I said to myself   I said   well
maybe I should talk about something   but I didn't learn
        anything
I couldn't talk about anything there was
lots of distraction today
A beautiful day   Lots of distraction   It had to do with
all these people all these too-many people
passing through my days and nights   But I
don't get to hear about ideas anymore   know what I mean
Just for the hell of it   Talking about ideas
takes the mind one step further
further than what it already knows   Doesn't
need to affirm itself   It's one step beyond affirming itself

Vulnerable   in a way that doesn't threaten
even weak people   Those nice-guy routines
They come up to you
because they know how to be a nice guy

Committing Sideways

This might hurt a bit, stabbing away at conversation
when we could be quiet or snoring, I mean
waking up sick is tomorrow's business (we like to say
that it wears our clothes). But what's substantial
is the soulful intersection of the needs and obligations
of good friends ridiculing each other. It's a chance

we don't hesitate to take, and we're a shambles,
aren't we? These arms don't work anymore. Better stack them
over here, where the suntans fell off our faces. And yes,
that's the old philodendron walking out in your slippers,
but forget it, it's nothing, the whole place and its aura
of lived-in azaleas are resting on tentative sand.

Funny little murmurs of free fall. Now we're
getting somewhere, so close and, therefore, so disappointed,
like slaphappy derelicts leaning on parking meters
after the shoppers have thinned away, and yet from them
emanates an excited kind of trust that can also turn inside out
and make visible what has remained so secret.

And we each say, "Well, here's to you, bub," as the last
jokes collide with the things we most
despise in ourselves, which march across the table like crummy
peanut-butter sandwiches in Day-Glo trench coats—whoops,
there they go—right through the breathy curtains,
right past the worry that we may be anything but

deadly serious when they return to us, as they always do,
when we're alone, and that our having to think about them
will hold us too safe and too separate, our feet
squarely planted in dreaded plots of ground.

Falling Behind

Falling behind, I was trying to hold on
to a stray branch stuck in the grass, a crowd of
bathrobes in a driveway, a missing gatepost
to alter the day, making it bearable. But as I drew closer
their difference loosely spread
through neutral streets, grey autumn, the way
ground fog or sadness gathers this city—
cold around the edges seeping in like rain through sleep.

People go on. Countless footsteps
pass through car doors, wind up stairs, and arrive
at far corners right on time. The victories there:
conversation. The calm strangers. The most available identity.
I couldn't know what doesn't change must be done
over and over again. I was thinking hard, chipping away
at my heart, unattaching a string of
birds from the wires, and disregarding them.
Each sound and nerve end
gives in to the dull sirens supporting the distance,
sounds in a memory without the memory's story.
The sighing, indecisive breeze
accumulates in the grave that was opened the day I was born.

Fir trees wander through the afternoon.
I was catching up with myself. Here's the newspaper,
the packets of Kasseri and Feta.
There's the drugstore's clean tile, the J & M card room,

the butcher's red flag. I was watching the woman
who snagged her sweater on the table.
I wanted to leave. I was already letting go.

Transient News

Well, fidgeting strangely, I woke up.
You see, I spent the night with Laura
because Laura's husband was out looking
for Laura. Toast and melon—she
poured the coffee, and I had to tell her
that I dreamed I was Ricky Ricardo.
"Some things they just go down
that way," she said, "even in America."

By then, I knew the tourists
had infiltrated Jackie's Odds & Ends.
Copped the newspaper. Tried to coerce
an aged couple into spotting me twenty
for showing them the brighter side
of their quarrel. The gentleman half
flinched his eyebrows and dreamed
he was the pubescent child in the candy aisle.
I was transferring items
from my left to my right rear pocket.
What can a poor fool do? Join
the Air Force? Wage war in Omaha?
This is a lovely town all right, like
a postcard, but you can't look at it forever.

I don't know. I should still
feel proud of myself, cordial, a regular
businessman during the eviction hearings.
Me and the landlord, we struck a deal.

Bitter? Nah, even left a lamb chop
on the cooler, and when the landlord
thought to call for keys, I took the time
to send them. Weeks later,
he lost the building.
Flies live there now.

Well, we could wait all afternoon for the bus,
and I think we have. The guy on the bench
straightens his nylons before striking
a melancholy pose. The lawyer
used to be a priest, the nurse has been married
five times, and the baker, he secretly
hates sugar. So I turn again
to the schoolgirl. She's so fat and pretty and shy,
and seems so fatalistic. I don't know,
but as I squeeze through to the back
of the bus, it's the whole tragedy
of everything being so unchangeable
and tired.

Fragile Hardware

Phone call...stacks of something
on top and in the drawers of all the desks...
I think a thing done is a similar time of day, and all day long
the sun rattles our fragile hardware.
In the heart of the city, the window glare that becomes
each building is a door, and that door is closing.

I wanted romance to be a start. Right here, in the harsh open.
We show up for work, grow tired, isn't that
enough? Eyeliner, the silken ties, we were making things easier,
and walking down Grand Ave. or drinking coffee at Pasquini's,
we want to hear about so-and-so, who did such and such,
who did it again.

Rustling time like this, sharing a little necessary
agitation. Now let's mess up the surface,
knock a few colors around, avoid the scene of which we're
so obviously a part. Yeah you've heard my complaints before.
You didn't think it could be done.
Do I understand your question?

So much you already know ...
No one was for extravagance, but getting by
has come to feed us, and it puts us to bed.
In Pershing Square, a man falls to his knees
for all the wrong reasons. Outside the bank, a woman pulls
her fingers through her hair. She pulls harder.

Between Two Tracks

Between two tracks of boxcars, closeness
is a clear eye, far from the crushed stones
that admit to nothing, maintaining a railroad.
They're all empties, doors open, and to look into one
introduces a confusion that lingers
and becomes another part of the protected space.
Warm hands in warm pockets.

At the waterfront the tracks are clearer.
Everything is twilight. The blue, flecked metal
illuminates the threads of my overalls. I want to ask
of the outstretched rails, of the utility poles,
their slow fan over Washington Street, Marion Street.
But their decisions have already been made.

The yellow blear of a taxi. Its wind lifting
the particular debris of our happiness:
playing card, paper cup, fake eyelash
trailing cool shadows to the water.
The zillion bubbles singing,
filtering upward like ghosts of flowers
that bloom on the slanted surface and stop singing.

Until pointless, I imagine I can go on
hearing them, calmly, up Western Ave.
The crosswalk beneath the bridge is dark
before the darkness fills it. The faraway sounds
of old things loosening unease me

like reluctant portions of too much I have hidden
stirring in my thickest skin. In the doorway
of Bob's Corner Café I wonder how long
it will take to focus. I hear a cough

and the rasp of a lighter. Somebody laughing. The blur
of small talk. I think about my nerves,
the strangeness and predictability of not wanting
to die here with a Tuesday-night special: ox tails
and dry rice, dabbed with gravy.
The warm air, of detergent and grease. My favorite table.
My favorite dark corner.

Recurring Motel

Already, the tired shoulders of the sofa
are nervous and discover how sleep becomes
another dark moment. The last gleams
of your head-oil vanish through the dull
stains of other fevers. Even the headache,
that was born from the cry, breaks down;

and your heart fills with the tilted lampshade,
starched towels, and subterranean folk songs of
names engraved on the tables. There is a need
to protect yourself, to unfasten the cold and believe
you have taken the hardest road to this motel.
You think about rising up and falling to the bed,

and you forget. At your feet, a package of
cigarettes and a shirt with a butterfly collar
grow small. The thin light of morning pales
and flattens the windows. Outside, the finches
are shy, chirping.

By Degrees

Nothing moves easily
outside the swamp of daydream. Nobody dries off in time.
The cold digs in like unwelcome memory,
knee-deep, with a club in its hand.

If there's really something to eat
let's put our cards on the table and be done with it.
The need that stays inside poisons the wilderness,
stirs my tar, and I'm out
trying to make miracles of anything that might happen.

If love can't be collision, then nothing
is forgiven, and we're just hanging around here
wasting our difference.

Untitled

for Rothko

Where the green landscape
naturally grows darker, out there,
near the orange building,
only the green is visible
in that orange space,
nothing but orange in that green.

★

We might pass through
those edges of skylight at night
and welcome the vague
activity we catch up to—
always in motion,
in the process of leaving, and

leaving. Sometimes, when
I'm really old, the balcony
too is a dream. Storms
of surrounding shape
are afloat on the eye's ocean,
just this far from shore.

★

Even the ugly spasms of
self-pity are lost

to the symmetry of distance.
In my coldest fire
of solitude, when all the world
is that horizon,

my heart unfolds a trail, splitting
the grey, icy soil
from the darker vault of echoes,
though nothing, nothing
that keeps me out and nothing that
I create, keeps me.

*

We dance through the hours. Your yellow
dress and my violet
breath whirling until, exhausted,
we sense the quiet sigh
in our bouquets of pale laughter.
And like the tiny

scar along the edge of your ear
that calls forth the pain
we never quite shared, being here
and the way in which
we're feeling here, require strangely
that we feel this way.

Earl Never Loses

Each evening the oldest
card player in the White Ace Hotel
deals poker
against a bottle of gin. His opponent,
his partner, burns holes through
his stomach and sends the red animal
scurrying. But Earl never loses.
Half shrugging, he piles the patriotic chips
on his side of the table, apologizing
to the losers—his old friend Bubba,
and Red-Eye, and Slim.

He delights in squashing
cigar butts in the tin plate of
diced meat and corn,
in getting so fired up
that he stumbles, slipping farther
from the roar and click of
night streets, receding
still inward upon his indolence,
fashioned by warm breathings of decay.
It's usually the black maid
who discovers him face-down
on the vinyl tablecloth, and she cradles

his colorless head
as she helps him to the cot.

But tonight, mysterious knuckles
rouse his eyelids.
Earl figures it is the knock
of a new, youthful challenger
though he's unable to conjure strength
in the tiniest of his drunk fingers.
Yellow, thick lamplight
burns his eyes with the ridiculous
smirk on the lip of his shot glass—
a dream of witnessing
his own sudden birth, shocking him
out of his life. And later,
another dream, a way of
cursing everything.

Long after the stranger has disappeared
down the hallway, Earl awakens, though
the knocking persists, rhythmically,
like a code to be broken.

Without looking at his cards, Earl knows
this is a hand to bluff with.
He closes his eyes, a signal he is not
at home, and smiles, holding his breath
until he is forgotten.

Not to Reach Great Heights, But to Stay Out of Great Valleys

There's a wind in the leaves of the trees.
It's a river of bone chips and feathers.
And the visible stars, in their airy
chasms, are fishes. I am kissing fishes.

I'm on my way to your place.
Do you hear my footsteps on the stairs,
and feel my cold lips
on your cheek? I am saying, "Hello, friend."

A few neighbors huddle on the corners
with upturned collars and turned-out
pockets. The blue smell of metal and
night things—an old gal snoozes with cans,

a bearded boy embraces a telephone pole.
And they're shooting each other, again,
at Los Globos. Splinters of bone
fall from the window like fish scales.

The band of spectators rises ecstatically.
They're the cause of their own
good fortune, they believe, but the lie
is like the crime itself, with its excuses.

"Hello, friend," I am saying
on top of the hill. You are wearing

stockings and slippers and a few sweaters;
it's always so cozy in your kitchen.

Have the pipes finally choked?
The ceilings are leaking. The stairwell
and hallway are lined with cake pans;
there are puddles everywhere. A puddle of

light has formed beneath your door. Ah, good.
I want you to be there. Are you there?

Back Down

I don't want to end here,
my head turned interminably
toward white and black shadows
prolonged behind a veil of eucalyptus trees.
End here. Like an office desk
or file cabinets, or keeping my head in order to respond
properly to a memo.
Oh, to get out of bed
and wash, only to be dragged
back down by the hands of somebody else's ritual.
To kneel before a sour notion of older days.
To surrender. To make money.

I want to know what you're doing now,
whether the work is dull or if, at least,
it goes well. And I'm thinking
of a dress you might be wearing, your fragrant shoulders,
the solitary water of your ancient calm.
A calm deeper than grief or boredom, distracting
a soul uprooted, hour by hour,
from the living bone.
So call me.
And whatever you do,
don't call, don't test me, you can't win.
If something creaks in the hallway,
if something winces or cracks under pressure
it belongs to you, and all my sincerity

is a hostile afternoon.
Don't call me. There's a meeting at four,
a report to be memorized, the pipes
gurgle and hiss and sound too important,
and I want you to call me,
I need to try to answer—
half sitting, half standing in the way of my life.

Cyclone Off the Coast

It's not so much the heat from the sun
and colors flooding the weird, rickety horizon,
or the heat-warped air over limp flags and bright brick,
where an ordinary sigh breeds what's right,
while the hard-core are properly disposed of
on the far-reaching hills. Cut and dry. Summer
sunbelt. No, nothing moves, and when Mrs. Flannigan
sees her son splash into the back-yard fountain
she hears nothing. And the gardener,
Fletcher, palpates a burned forehead before clipping
the hedge his partner just finished.
And the clouds high, so high in the sky—
who can account for the day
they arrived here, and why they won't go away?

Nighttime comes, and for what? The wee hours?
Bits of steam oozing up from the ruined streets,
street cleaners and thumping wharf rats,
the well-lit places, the false drug
that can't help the night, though it repaints
the angular expressions of a dead decade;
and for the losers not even passing out assures sleep
when the hushed chill changes the guards,
when their eyes loosen the burden of remembering;
and the memory, like the pain that is our distance,
shrugs the dawn with excessive heat, latent
and inclined to be its own source—ready when you are—

ripping up trees and tearing out hair, leaping
from bridges: a house whirling, a man whistling
in the azygous muscle, the rumpled wind.

Ground Glass

We were going round and round
until it must be the day before
that passes through our understanding of
hazy skies in the apartment windows

across the alley. And the light recalls neighbors
fixing breakfast, rearranging furniture,
opening and closing doors to what we take
most for granted: where we are,

where food and a bed and some of
our friends are, the hum of the city
and the time, subliminal, moving away
from the two o'clock of this day.

So, we're off in that direction. There's
the one shoe out ahead, and the shoe
that lags behind us—even the pale
obscure details of commitment may be trusted.

(The veritable green clouds. A pigeon,
cooing the air conditioner. Pockets. Brief pause.
Side-glance. Those who, upon entering,
declare a stiff wind down the hallway.)

Yes, we might hold the comfort, but to know that
is to feel how much commitment can never be enough.

Nobody is hungry, and everyone sits
at the table; no meal has been prepared, though

the napkins are politely unraveled.
And again, the present arrives without form.
The gloom, which has crept in, stays,
while desire fills the spaces between you

and the rest, making them real obstacles.
Everything is out of reach, jabbing the center
with the intensity of a touched-off mob.
Protection watches over its own body:

some of this nervousness feels good, pumped-up,
backing you into the hidden red brick,
into the same old story you shout
from the shadows of too much. A few people

turn and look, though they may not
have heard you, their faces are clearer,
hard-edged. A child pulls at his mother's blue
jacket and bends over backwards, his mouth

wide open, his eyes in the vertical sky.
At the corner a man stumbles through the crowd,
pushing another man into somebody else.
They all apologize, but you can't help worrying

about that ancient woman leaning on the bus stop,
so undeniably calm. And it's all right,
the way it comes to be understood, walking
along the avenue, with the others, to a later hour.

Secretive, But Honest

And the clouds are calling,
calling out to the waves of wheat
that break over the clouds.
Always, there is a wooden fence.
Always, the small stones
like footprints,
like men who are lost,
men who know that they are lost.
The stones are a reminder,
though they too
are out of the picture.

★

It's not so easy to be born
right now. Cold season,
and the scarf is outside of me.
These boots are outside of me
and all this breath, the heartaches,
dead squirrels.
All this breath. All the days and all
the nights endow each sublime object,
each source of new direction.
We can only want what we need,
each useless thing, each other life.
Another shadow on a dimly lit wall

· buttering toast in the steam of his coffee.
Nothing is really where it is.

★

I confess to knowing the whereabouts
of what you want from me. You are so easily pleased,
but to please, unfortunately,
is not a young detective's responsibility.
Even as we are the guilty parties, I will not
accept that kind of power. Each forage
locates the same pale hands, choking
the victim's laughable,
his pitiful and his wide-eyed, his nearly dead.
It is time, I think,
to live up to the price we pay.

City Country

"There was something particularly
funny about this photograph, but I seem
to have misplaced it," he said, in the last
quarter hour of the week in which two years of
his life boiled down to a few, nasty cusswords
strung together in new patterns—brilliant, almost floral,
like the orangish-green wallpaper he grew up with.
You know, some roosters doting over
some chickens. Some eggs. Or fences.
"We got bigger," he said, over and over again.

"I'm going home now," he said,
where the freeway bends from west
to north to the building shapes in the pastel healing.
Yes. A little time to call his own—
billboard or play field—and the feeling seemed
awake forever. And the feeling worse
awakened the outstretched spirit
flung over those foothills like clouds along elegant,
rocky pathways to the only funeral in any town.
Yes. Window. And the window
is properly locked.

"I remember Larry," he said, "walking
through the yard, stopping before the pear tree
or willow. He climbed the thin branches
in the way we used to do it at dusk—

quietly, with the moist cold.
We would see the lake from there,
and the grey island that seemed to look back at us;
and we would find the blue from there,
and the blue gradations of green.
It wasn't giving up really. Nothing much changed.
We, mostly far away."

Anxious Latitudes

Up here, I am hyperactively farsighted.
My brain weighs three pounds and
when the show got on the road
my body was a mere appendage of it.

On a clear day, I'm busy directing landscapes,
not really shoving the shrubs around,
not ordering pastel houses from the hillsides,
but carrying them with me like a frayed

photograph in my wallet, so that I might read it
as a small corner of its vaster itinerary.
How the background shows through, blank smudges
and the so many time-connecting dots,

with all I've come to expect deferred to some
higher order, place or pocket watch ticking together,
both of this world and on that side of the fence.
By now, judging from here,

the rewards must be enormous. Though
my body weighs as much as fifty brains,
always doing, always feeling, mostly feeling
(to get gushy), the traffic bangs and

snarls around me, and the collapsed pause
absents all passing scenery before it moves on,

now farther away. This happens every yesterday
and pained expressions linger on our faces.

We can be thankful for that, each one dying
to talk with somebody, just the two of us
bringing it all home, putting together
the movable parts on their merry way.

But time is short, only twenty minutes (we have
the sandwiches to eat) until the loudest voice
coheres as many, lacquering the politics
of company policy, and its words greet us

not with love, but from fear
that repeated toil simply hardens the argument
that work is all there is, like the whistle
signaling a return to designated places.

So when the paychecks are spooned out, I'll take mine
as if to tell you, "O.K., you're right!
You're the victor, now write the history, please."
You see, I don't even know what clothes

I'm wearing, whether or not they are comfortable
or stylish. Just too nervous to care
and I'm on an extended vacation,
sweating in the balance.

from *Neither World*

Long Shadows, Many Footsteps

And so, another cover bursts into flames.
And so, even nakedness
is only a symbol of doors opening.

This isn't a city, but a forest.
And a child on an adventure who
happens by a stone farmhouse

(and is offered warm milk there)
thinks he'll return again
and bring his friends—how happy they'll be—

even as an hour later
he's running freakishly through night's
black leaves, lost, trying to fetch his dog.

And there are grown-ups
with somewhere to go
who just keep on walking;

they remember later the white sink,
the bathtub, in a fire-gutted tenement.
For people, other people

can't be enough. These aren't
the faces of friends, but faint, disturbing
webs of alliance, long-winded stories

that we listen to desperately
but can't understand. The woman
who comes to me thinks that making

love can break a person down
and get to what he knows, but there's
nothing really to show her.

And in the dream that recurs each night
the apartment door opens to the blue
of a blue sky, and Hanula isn't there,

isn't visible, but here, the way
the sound of sod on the blessed's cold wood
is here. I don't know, I can't imagine,

I don't know about death,
but am learning to bury my own kind.

Subliminal Birds

Like the infant, wriggling free, tasting air,
hollering from the blue cliffs of Echo Park.

Like clear wind, like ashes rising from the tips of leaves,
or wooden storefronts in the must of towering construction.
And all that occurs while waiting, or forgetting,
the sound of a train in the heart's distance.

All that coming and going, so much
life spreading its wings in both worlds,
soaring beneath the crust of the handshake and signature,
between the lines of stories we tell
in order to be heard here,
in order to feel confidently at home.

Right here, where walls of survival are windows.
A whole galaxy of stars in the nod of the proprietor
of a carnival shooting-gallery.
Where, ecstatically, with the blinds drawn,
a woman tumbles from her bed
into the swirling green waters of an Oriental carpet.

Where children, school kids
in grey and white uniforms, twirl
until the buildings
are dust on the parched lips of a storm,
a shimmering ribbon,
an indelible, radiant, haze.

Unspeakable

Summer has its way
around here. People kind of
cave in, weary
with the certainty of nighttime,
how it draws even these last
illusory shimmers of tropical ice
into its own oblivion.

And all the flowers
have withered away. The animals
too, are forgotten.
Now the pavement
keeps getting hotter.
City lights churn.
And out in those parking lots
and behind iron doors
your neighbors stare into their
billion broken mirrors.

A desire
perhaps to blame them,
to give them all new faces,
the ones you've painlessly
selected—brisk and cheerful—
until each prisoner's
freed from his imagined
demands, and all your hope
becomes your nature, out

among the lush foliage
of the future.

A desire to be noticed
perhaps, by the old guy
who rants in the stupid
glow of his icebox,
to show your scars
to the scowling landlady,
absolutely terrified
of lifting the lid of the dumpster,

to point them out,
to brush them aside with a laugh
and a wave of the hand
for the boy who
wanders these rooftops
each night, envying everyone
who can walk well enough
on the ground, even though
they're obvious and ordinary,

even though
what you'll finally speak of
does not belong to,
and no longer resembles,
your wound.

The River Has No Hair to Hold Onto

It's only common sense (not that they know the score,
they don't avoid it). And so one's life story
is begun on a paper napkin and folded into a coat pocket
to be retrieved later when it's darker
and cooler, and closer. And onward

to rockier ground, where conversation is impassable
and human beings matter more than
the light that glimmers beneath the horizon
before sinking into our own inaudible sigh (a long way
from these fur-covered hands). And somehow

the deal is struck. Money gets made.
And the small shocks one undergoes for no reason,
the bus driver handing you a transfer, a steamy
saxophone ascending the jungle. The city
lays down its blanket of rippling

lamplight as though exhaustion too
was achieved by consensus, and what one does
and how one feels have nothing to do with one's self.
No, this can't be the place, but it must be
the road that leads there, always beginning

where morning is slow and hazy, suffering to get somewhere
with all the memorable mistakes along the way,
piecing them together, arriving,

believing that one arrives at a point different from
the starting point, admitting things still aren't clear.

A rag doll on a dark lawn injures the heart
as deeply as the salt sea air filling one's lungs
with the sadness once felt in a classroom,
a sadness older than any of us.
And the dogs barking, challenging cars. And the willows

lining the sidewalk, lifting their veils
to the inscrutable surface of wood. (Someone
is trying to get a message through. Someone thinks
you'll understand it.)

The Privilege of Silence

No threats. Not the teaser
this time. Finally there is a random God.
And all the filthy laundry we've hung out to dry,
all the fingers we've grown used to pointing,
sneer, backbite, everything that worked
yesterday, nothing a little
breeze won't knock down.

Even wisdom, the pure heart, the woman
who for six days among impatient nurses
choked on water, who knew a full
life when she saw one, who never asked of anybody,
begged for air, was made
to beg for something
she knew she was en route to.

Only the living take things for granted.
The dead don't leave; some part of us
is missing. And we sense
the echo, the wind in our
veins, faces like thin
curtains that let in the light
and let loose our shadows.

Even asleep, in the ancient dance,
we are turning away.
Turning toward the ruckus
of jacarandas. A face in the crowd

that offers itself like early morning,
unknowingly, as we are drawn to it.
More strangely than that.

Leaving One

I don't want any numbers.
I'm worn out beforehand.
I don't care about
who's sleeping with whom.
I only know what people don't tell me,
how it's difficult to be a human being,
that the complication begins inside
the way loneliness can't be
located in any one part of the body,
that it rises from the surface
where the soul should be
and rears its ugly head
in the face of anything tender,
those fingers of yours, those knees.

You sit beside me at the window.
We are not drinking the coffee,
we don't eat the toast.
Outside, in the park, two huge maples
are ablaze with Indian summer,
and absolutely still.
People parade the sidewalks,
brush against one another at crossings.
No one needs to understand anything
to get the goods on everyone.
It's the way of morning,
a malicious, well-trained avoidance.

My staying here
would not protect you, these fingers
of yours, the soul in your shy eyes,
I'd simply go down trying.
We, right here, belong to us.
But I'm calling the shots now,
and now I'm leaving this hotel.
With all we've lost already
our pores are wide open.
And it's cold out there.
Come drive with me.

In Every Direction

As if you had actually died in that dream
and woke up dead. Shadows of untangling vines
tumble toward the ceiling. A delicate
lizard sits on your shoulder, its eyes
blinking in every direction.

And when you lean forward and present your
hands to the basin of water, and glimpse the glass face
that is reflected there, it seems perfectly at home
beneath the surface, about as unnatural
as nature forcing everyone to face the music
with so much left to do, with everything
that could be done better tomorrow, to dance
the slow shuffle of decay.

Only one season becoming another,
continents traveling the skyway, the grass
breathing. And townspeople, victims, murderers,
the gold-colored straw and barbed-wire hair of the world
wafting over the furrows, the slashed roads
to the door of your office or into the living room.

The towel is warm and cool, soft to the touch,
but in another dream altogether
a screen door creaks open, slams shut,
and across the valley a car's headlights swing up

and over. And maybe you are the driver
with both hands on the wheel, humming a tune
nobody's ever heard before,

or maybe the woman on the edge of the porch,
grown quiet from fleeing,
tough as nails.

Breaking and Entering

Many setups. At least as many falls.
Winter is paralyzing the country, but not here.
Here, the boys are impersonating songs of indigenous
wildlife. Mockingbird on the roof of the Gun Shop,
scrub jay behind the Clear Lake Saloon.
And when she darts into a drugstore for a chocolate-covered
almond bar, sparrow hawks get the picture
and drive off in her car.

Easy as 8th & Spring Street,
a five-course meal the size of a dime.
Easy as vistas admired only from great distance,
explain away the mystery
and another thatched village is cluster-bombed.
Everyone gets what he wants nowadays.
Anything you can think of is probably true.

And so, nothing. Heaven on earth. The ruse
of answers. A couple-three-times around the block
and ignorance is no longer a good excuse.
There were none. Only moods
arranged like magazines and bones, a Coke bottle
full of roses, the dark, rickety tables about the room.
And whenever it happens, well, it's whatever it takes,
a personality that is not who you are
but a system of habitual reactions to another
light turning green, the free flow of
traffic at the center of the universe where shops

are always open and it's a complete
surprise each time you're told that minding your own business
has betrayed your best friend. But that's over,
that's history, the kind of story that tends to have an ending,
the code inside your haunted head.

Easy as guilt. As waking and sleeping, sitting down
to stand up, sitting down to go out walking,
closing our eyes to see in the nocturnal
light of day. "Treblinka
was a primitive but proficient
production line of death," says a former *SS Untersharfürer*
to the black sharecropper-grandchild of slavery
who may never get over
the banality of where we look.

Only two people
survived the Warsaw uprising, and the one
whose eyes are paths inward, down into the soft grass,
into his skeleton,
who chain-smokes and drinks, is camera shy,
wears short-sleeved shirts, manages to mumble,
"If you could lick my heart, it would poison you."

At the Seams

When I think I see clearly and, therefore, think about thinking
    about,
let me be in the dark, measure and strain, let this old
bread stand for sustenance, I may choose not to eat it.
And when I think it's okay to sleep
or that memory's a comfort less malicious than
happiness, give me the courage
to deal these cards to the wind
and keep walking.

All day long the world sings to itself.
Buildings don't change color, don't
shimmy, they don't lie. But two people in the same room,
the one with a lump in her throat, the other changing
the channel, the five
billion lives that hang on their going through with it,
just like that, busting up some ceiling.

In the damp garden of faces our eyes
twitch like shooting stars, a stitch of
bone. Ghost vein, hinterland, echo-of-eternity, it takes
practice to get lost, paint with our own hair, burrow deeply
into shadows of flesh coming undone at the seams.
Over billowing grasses, fierce grasses,
a low branch settles for a handful of splinters.
Take more.
Take more than you can repay.

Veils of Prayer

When the sky darkens
and turns white, and the green
and blue leaves deepen—
showers of mist, bamboo, the lemons shine.
A light was left on, white azalea, I had left a light on for you.
Do not come back, not now. Though still here
I too can't return.

Only the edges
go on like this, long into dusk, the soul
drains us in seconds.
And the nothing that's left, and the no more
hope, and what I wouldn't
kill off or trade away, fuck over, dismiss, make a joke of, this
failure of solitude, my own dark
standing alone in the dark hand that feeds me.

Into this night . . . and drunker.
The drone of the crickets. Voices without mouths, without glare,
the fence just fading away, everything
and my own exhausted space,
to privacy.
          Into this night,
I swear it, years disappear without a voice of your own,
a middle ground, all those
reasons for giving in, for holding on, leaving

again and again,
to poison—all those islands of blame.

                              And ain't nobody lives there.
Trees high on the ridge. The laconic wires.
Lit windows and shutting down.
A sigh in the shrubs, on the porches, and shutting down.
When the sky darkens . . .
When the dark finds the needle . . .

Please. Not ever.
I'm still failing. Unforgiven. Alone.
That you can be right if you want to.
I won't recognize you.
That we may never be resolved.
That I may be at peace.
That I may heal into the husk of my heart.

Evolving Similarities

I know there are pigeons smaller than we are
roaming the parks and the alleys.
I have seen us go down lightly
and sideways
and get back home again one day at a time.
For people like us
there are pigeons everywhere.

I know moss-covered brick
and the short walk back to the studio.
I'm familiar with reclining nudes
and the orange goldfish.
In the dankest of circumstances
I too have dialed the number
and thought twice and tested each one of them

as if anybody stands a chance around here
and no one carries our messages.
If there's something you still need
believe me
they will pick up the phone.

Because the body's *not* stupid.
Because the flesh remembers
and taking care comes first.
A young mother cradles an infant to her breast

and it feels like love.
Like we can do something.

Because you would save every last one of them
you are already forgiven.
It doesn't matter now
that nothing in this world is direct.
Our life is layered.
First we weep
and then we listen and eat something
and weep again

and listen.
And eat again.
And it doesn't matter anymore
at the bottom of your story

at the very-most bottom of recovery.
And confession.
And then popped for it.
Even the one who's picked up unconscious
is resisting arrest.

And it just happens to be perfectly okay
to feel like you're understood.
They'll follow you anywhere.
They will peck at your shoes in the plaza.
A cluster of violets on the floor of the rain forest

pumping water
making food.

I know that dread is wrapped up in knowing.
I know the way dread tends to consume itself.
And I apologize
for just barely listening.
But if I cry tonight
tell me
who is there among us who will call your bluff?

Love's That Simple

At those who love you, who look up to you or just happen to
        feel like human beings
because of you. Even the moon would shed its skin,
the infant its shadow for you.

I mean you can if you want to,
in the face of, at whatever it is you think you can buy.
Money itself, or childhood, or somewhere to run to, someone
        impatient enough to speak for you.
You're no fool, you're entitled. And the only way
to avoid pain is to inflict it on somebody else.

But you *haven't* disappeared them,
though they're there for you. In gardens of sulfur, with
        blackened walls, until the heart is tamed and my lips bleed.
And intimacy, a taunt. And trust,
a stratagem. Your mama's racism.
Your daddy's legalese.

Here are the spiders that will crawl through your eyes.
Passion. Resilience. The wild, cold colors
of the Mediterranean. What if all you can do is despise
what you came for? The flawless. The seamless.
You've invented everyone!

Talk to them. What they think about and feel.
What they'll do the next time.

You, who are not responsible, chased by nothing, who limp
            nowhere. Tell them
about the mountain and the kingdom within.

And resentment. Betrayal. You had such high hopes for them.
The no one who takes a back seat to you,
who won't live up to whatever it was,
it's just too complicated.

We either forgive one another who we really are
or not.

At Your Convenience

Whether it blew up in your face
or on television. From the driver's seat, into just about
any household. Most of the sink is there,
and the plumbing beneath it.
The cabinet.
Part of a wall.

Whatever sold the paper, kicked ass,
Thank God, in the courtroom. Where it's
hidden in a hospice, an old folks home, as if you've
done yourself a favor this time.
Not even children breathe around here.

Into what language does the raised voice disappear?
Which alphabet will throw open
the shutters, add on a couple of more rooms,
Thank God, and pee in the roses, lose its footing,
and go on dancing?

Tonight, the neighbors are breaking up furniture.
They are breaking bottles and kicking cans
and circling the block.
Tonight, the neighbors scream into plastic bags,
so maybe you're right, nobody's
yelling at you.

And so what? Even thinking about it
is an example of tears—as if the question in the air tonight
is How do I deal with this problem?—
already crystallized, faked out by experience,
perfected, adorned.

In front of everyone. Deep down,
and rid of.
Not that you don't know what they're saying.
You do. You know what they're talking about.
Not that there ever was a problem.
It's just that you disagree.

Headlights Trail Away

and go on surprising. It happens.
Everything. A couple of suitcases
falling from a fourth-story apartment—
fertilize the African violets
and there you have it, new slippers
in the hallway—the relentless, invisible
moon of my heart, hugging its orbit.

Yes, it's raining,
or about to. Black splotches
on the sidewalk. Gum wrappers
in a gutter stream. I feel I've
changed so many times in the last
fifteen seconds that the cold
must belong to the fishwoman's
darker eye, sparrows in the hollow
of a traffic light.

All else is habit, like believing
you're right, you're a decent, good person.
It's the same street, no matter
what punches are thrown, the same
signs. A house of cards
with a barber stropping the razor
and the janitor jangling keys,
with packages to wrap, the several breezes.
There is the faintest trace of basil

on the breath of the waitress.
It tickles, that taste,
and what can you do?
Such a pleasure to be here.

Among Fields of Shocked Corn

And what about what the slow
undulation of farmland
is doing to the sky?
There is one quiet cloud there
keeping the world at bay,
tearing itself apart.

Sugar maples. Red oaks.
The hardwoods are the most
fragile, a shivering beauty,
the long fall to dirt heaven.
I know now how a farmhouse
was the invention of distance.
The hay is rolled, the silos
gleam as if there's
something left worth saving.

And the old farmer
on his tractor, plowing
salt into the furrows
so that a man might never get up,
stand on his good two feet,
sleep with his wife, and
walk away again.
I own less and less
of myself. I rented

this sucker to get out of town,
and now I want to drive up
onto that median and
turn it around. I have one last
favor to ask of just about
everyone: whatever you do,
don't confuse Ralph Angel
with Ralph Angel. Today,
he loves everything too much.

And I want it simple,
a small breath filling the world
with tremendous music.
Among fields of shocked corn
you are stepping into your car.
Stranger, my love, you really are.
Place your hands on my chest.
You can trust me.
See, they go right through.

A Rat in the Room

What a guy goes through these days
to get his uncle Leo to pass him a couple of lentils!
Every twisted crime of the century. All manner of jugular
and spit. "You're a loser, kid."

Then the sun goes down. A fork
whizzes by. How could I have imagined it,
my hands around his throat, this jumping up and down?
I thought that might make us closer. Everything out on the table,
enough to drive you crazy, a guy could
kill someone!—until a vase of snapdragons is knocked over

and the pot roast lands on cousin Regina,
until, finally, the cauliflower, the Brussels sprouts
are ridiculous, the way the truth can be ridiculous
whenever it's finally found.

And that's it. The worst
and best times. Billboards and lightning,
black trees in a rear-view mirror
and out of this life. Another five minutes alone
and I won't be able to keep myself company,
like a security guard patrolling
expensive homes, taking from them the framed
and pampered objects, not just to get himself busted
but because having been caught will make him more interesting.

Some part of me downs a stiff one
and knows too well his miserable moment of euphoria.
And a side I've had some luck in hiding
rifles the medicine cabinet before losing consciousness.
Sometimes, you have to be a totally different person
looking over his shoulder, back at you,
in order to see what it is you're up to.

An insomniac's light
flicks on in a neighbor's apartment, and old-man Riley
paces his living room. He smokes
a Marlboro. And another.
He punches the channel selector of his remote control.
With a scalpel, a disgruntled alien
is stabbing a patient. Riley jacks up the volume.
First the legs, then the face, the breast,
the back of the neck. And one by one,

everybody in the building is awake.
The creaking floorboards. Small
shudders in the plaster. Miss Julie, the hairdresser,
sprawls over a chair, sharpening nails.
Aroma of reheated coffee.
The Murphy's think they're hungry, grease the skillet
for a tall stack of sweet-and-sour flapjacks.
And the ancient, most honorable, Mrs. Costello
pokes her head out a ground-floor
bedroom window, looking tired
and skyward. "Is somebody gonna do me a favor
and shut that nut up?"

Old-man Riley, he can't sleep.
It's what he wanted.

Breaking Rhythm

And then the head is at odds with the body.

And then the head strangles your way of thinking.

But don't get me wrong. It's not
that I'm saying life's taking us nowhere,

if I'm not saying *yes*, I'm a liar, a liar who does not
dwell in the shadow of his own home—

kind of your average, respectable, two-bit junkie who thinks he
    knows what he's after,
and what he's after is nightmare. Concussive. Brutal. The unending
ritual of eluding detection rising up and taking
shape with flaring nostrils and enormous hands,

and if it just happens to be pain that he's in right now,
well, at least, pain is who he is for a while.

No big deal. Out loud
the pulse quickens and, very loudly, prolongs itself.

Anger slams the door on a mettlesome friend of a friend,

and then I am boredom paying for groceries,
most happy when you chew on my chin
in luxurious sweat, in our sexual oil,

exhaustion on the subway back to the city. The fact is
I can only hear one part of myself at a time.

And it's late. And I'm tired. And it sounds like
all or nothing. A fistful of thirst and a cup of hot tea,

the silence shame gathers into no boundary.

The robe. The pocket knife. The loaves of bread.
Mud on the carpets. The shatter of leaves.

The wonder, the wonder, the wonder.

Untitled

Surely everyone is born unfinished,
could use a great deal of life today, and dies enough,
enough to keep the wound from healing.

And a cry comes close. A siren
cuts across it. It's the dying that torments us,
taking something and in a hurry

as if it were a beauty that one couldn't bear,
taking something more. Surely everyone
suffers to the knees of the heart

when the heart is open.
And I don't recover. A cry
cuts across it. The red camellias cut across it

where rain drips from the eaves,
drums the stepping stones after a storm has
cleared the face of everything: porches

and cancer, pine trees, the bird on the white wing.
And the neighborhood blind dog. Little dwarf,
half hairless, half lame, punishes

the curb, the treacherous ivy. Our little
neighborhood comedian. Choke chain, chest puffed out,
yaps at the air, yapping the length of ultimate

driveways, sideways, backwards, until
another dog barks back. Look out! Each step
a shock of joy.

Getting Honest

What goes down in the course of a day
means nothing to me, it means
nothing to me.
It's everything in the world to me.

One minute I'm on my way back to the city
and I hear myself say
that I'm not going to let it bother me. And I don't,
and it's over—wholly arbitrary.
I could have let it destroy me.
At any other moment I probably would have.

Right now he's thinking about all and anything.
It's a way of avoiding everything. "Don't worry," he says,
"I knew you were lying."
And maybe I was. Out there
it goes badly for me.

And the Grass Did Grow

Nothing is happening,
and yet what is being acted out
or proven right now, flamboyantly,
might just turn a corner
and become the real thing.

Mostly holed up in a room
somewhere, or pacing the twilit
underworld of the neighborhood,
another honest display of emotion taking up
its fair share of available space,
and all the desire I can possibly
imagine, like a stone flung,
inscribing its arc of air.

But living is fickle, open-ended,
even the little myths break down.
Nobody thinks I'm very funny.
In fact, they're insulted.
They've exacted their portions
and now appear rather chipper,
scattering me over the hillsides

and into the night.
Like a pedestrian in a crosswalk
replaced by another man, I go with them.
And I don't go. The need remains
forever: to have, to get my hands on,

or to be taken, to lose myself
in a warmer, less urgent caress.

I open one eye, take a look around.
No pat answers, no permanence or rest.
Someone just happens to keep beginning,
and my life too, where I left it,
over there.

The Blessed

There is a place, I swear it,
where sadness fits, but with all this blood on our hands
we choose what to do and make ourselves up.

Ask anyone, and get an answer.
The salsa's on aisle five, next to the dust mops.
Cracked vases and damp hallways—

it's a purely private life. The way
taking it easy is absolutely
full-time. The sign-language

of windows and doorways, of a man watching a woman
who's watching another man throw down a broom.
Even your faint, familiar voice,

muffled and thirsty,
until its sheer impossibility
moved me over, and I could hear you.

And in this desert of moss, and mountains,
we eat raisins, olives, eggs,
because what is solid

has no opening,
like mourners who have no mouths,
and cannot object, and will remember forever.

Shadow Play

She leaves the motor running.
I would too. I would like to marry her,
that face repeated a million times in this town.
In the exhaust next door a man twists
his wooden leg into an impossible position.
He doesn't even have to say, "I know,
I know, and nobody resents me."
He just grins.

On the vendor's tin scales, daylight
shifts and splinters. Blood on the black brick,
a shopkeeper sweeps glass from his eyelids.
A young man fidgets in a doorway,
cups his hands around a blue
flicker of panic, and leans back
into the shuffling papers and footsteps,
the noise that opens away from him
and is not noise.

Now a cleaning lady stops herself
and looks over her shoulder. And so does
the mailman, a traffic cop, a kid walking his bike.
And the perfect word lodges
deep in the throats of businessmen
talking gibberish, drawing lines around themselves
until obsessed and hailing taxis.
Only our loose clothes

between us, the linen tablecloths, white
as blindness. Only the putter of canal boats,
the vine-covered walls, some cursory
glance that empties our eyes, when they meet,
of options, and won't let go.
A person who might

grow older. People who will dash their dreams.
People who will come back and
live in the aroma of bread, in the sound of
a thousand doves unfolding the plaza.
I would like a glass of ice water.
It's the little thing, when I'm lucky
the world comes to me.

from *Twice Removed*

Twice Removed

Not even sleep (though I'm ashamed of that too).
Or watching my sleeping self drift out and kick harder, burst
        awake, and then the nothing,
leaf-shadow, a shave and
black coffee, I know how a dream sounds.

This ease. This difficulty. The brain that lives on a little longer.
        The long
commute (not even what happened back then—this sort of
giving up with no one around and therefore
no charge for anything).

No word. No feeling
when a feeling wells up and is that much further.
Cupola and drumming, from the inside, holes open up a sky
        no thicker than cardboard.
You, the one I'd step over. You, whom I care for

and lie to, who doesn't want to, either, not even this failure
(having grown so used to it), the wreck that still
seeps from a stone, sinks down among the roots and, in that
        perfect darkness, such bloom.
No name for it. No place inscribed with its own grief,

where the grass resists, and I too

resist.

No place to get to. No place to leave from. No place where
       those times,

and times like these, are allowed to die.

Months Later

Where? In the black trees that lay down and drown here? In
the drowned clouds?—and no one to hold them back.
Rhododendron, the night never ends. A still-life and a
way to get home again. A moss-dark photograph
turned holy in his memory.

It's anyone against the wind tonight. In the eyes of a child who
looks up at us from the bottom of a well, or across the
table, the uninvited guest taking the oranges we
intended to eat.

In these very hands. A window of the soul already open to the
sea. An hour outside of itself. A name that's repeated
over and over until it's just noise.

River of ashes. River and flame, the small vibration we set in
motion there. I wouldn't know how to find you or
anyone.

Searchlights and choppers. With cats on the rooftops and
moths-turned-to-dust on the sill. Pillar, and bell
tower. Wall, and earlier than that, the peaceful cities.

Calm, without talking. In our oldest clothes. From the balcony,
on the fire escape—just leaning on the railings above
the flooded streets.

The Nothing That Is

That there was later on
among the tables and the tents of swirling light
the most exotic chill of laughter,
wrists, and touchable,
the need to touch and hear the distance,
umbrella damp, the last few
ugly words come back to pain
already lifted.

Not answering.
Not answering and, therefore,
not alone, double-fisted, this public
alley, this private wooden desk and room,
the cards and letters
I'm afraid of.

That there was later still,
but briefer, another cover, another
leap of faith and most of us, the untouched
sand and ether. Not you,
but blankly. Not her,
the looping swallows, the muffled eaves.
In the liquid light of traffic,
jasmine, cough and shatter. The hand
pressed close.
The mere sensation.

The Local Language

The way she puts her fingers to his chest when she greets him.

The way an old man quiets himself,

or that another man waits, and waits a long time, before speaking.
It's in the gaze that steadies, a music

he grows into—something about
Mexico, I imagine, how he first learned about light there.

It's in the blank face of every child,
a water that stands still amid the swirling current,

water breaking apart as it leaves the cliff and falls forever
through its own, magnificent window.

The way a young woman holds out a cupped hand, and doves
        come to her.

The way a man storms down the street as if to throw open every
        door.

And the word she mouths to herself as she looks up from her
        book—for
that word, as she repeats it,

repeats it.

Late for Work

In the throes
of winter a tropical storm muddies
the gutters

where traffic congests and then as always
eases us through.

Maybe I knelt there
for since they have vanished the lamps
in shop windows

flicker within. Somebody
flinching. A red
umbrella and that part of town swept from the hip

and the shoulder.
From my

open side. Somebody
pushing a bicycle. Somebody's alone
on the square.

So much
springtime we slog to catch up
to that first wave

of heat. People chatting
and murmuring. A young man

pouring tea.
The way an old man dabs his wet face
with a napkin. The way

she reclines when she reads.
So much cinnamon
and bread.

God how I love Darjeeling.

Breathing Out

Now you are crossing a wide street at night
anxious in the traffic and rushing
to get to the bakery
before closing. What could be more breathtaking
than your beauty if not in my arms
at least on that side
of peril. That's
why I'm yelling at the driver of the pickup truck
I just slammed into so much did I
want to park there and
wait for you.

May I never live with love
by surviving love and loving blocks and days away
the most ancient of the dead desire earthly
our getting born again
alone without
choice

children fill the air
the spices and the rugs of the bazaar.

I buy you tulips.
They are yellow and bright.
The port is dark and glittering blue airplanes
hover there. Like clarity
itself. Like
faintly wailing sirens attached to absolutely

nothing.
Like socks and sweaters and
the blanket that slipped somehow
from your legs while I
tidied up the balcony so lost in your book
are you tonight.

Even Because

Because it all just breaks apart, and the pieces scatter and
    rearrange without much fanfare or notice.

Because you can't and don't remember the step that kicked up dust
    and left this planet—you'd give up even more now.

Because the body itself—the heart's

not dead but deeper, wrapped up in curtains, a different color,
    among the railings and the pigeons, the rooftops and
    walls—

for all you know it's a question of bread

or beer.

Because even love

returns. The city's all brightness

and shadow, deckle-edged, bluer than air—there's no help
    anywhere—you no longer know how to listen.

And love says, love—midnight to midnight,

already ablaze. And the boulevard—wide-open. And the well-
    stocked crowdless market, and a lone taxi blears.

Even happiness—the way anger's come back to roost again.
  And joy, though joy's not in the ear or the eye. On
  this walk

the gulls hover off shore and the islands are speckled with fire.

Even love, even because.

Untitled

A poem begins.
People are walking down the street.
A few of them step into a doorway and light cigarettes.
A silhouette turns in a hotel-lobby window toward your
      reflection.
Everything hurries to make room for you.
You and all those you love and no longer know or grieve for
      and wish were here.
Enters your room and sits down.

A stick figure tosses a hat from the bridge.
A girl child crawls out of a cardboard box and cracks herself
      up.
Two hands clapping.
Is there not among the tables a waiter

already there?
The hollow sound of waves and a shopkeeper sweeping?
A woman dining alone?

They say that these scarves are among the finest in the world.
The purest water anywhere.
Adorn yourself.
Luxuriate.
The birds have fashioned the trees.
From a bench in the shade a couple looks out from a dream.
Vendors of ice cream

and baskets.

It is your eyes they look into.

Even the one who closes his own to hear himself singing.

Untitled

Or as along the river buildings brighten and grow dim again.
As a distant bridge repeats itself, and the domes above, and that
    much further, the city reassembled there.

Easy as listening, or choosing not to. A breeze comes up, a
    door glides
through its own perfect outline. Halyards and traffic. In a
    courtyard the puddles of last night's rain.

I watched my pain ease between spaces of the air itself.
Watched a waiter fidget with his apron, a woman selling lilacs,
    arranging cans. Strangers, their footsteps, as if

the soul were buoyed there, moist and leafy, a shadowed street
    where fruit rots in a wooden crate.
A pile of bricks. A ladder. Packages and papers, I miss everyone.

As in this quiet, always. My body. A whispered song.
As if, in this quiet, a man turns away and with a pole a
    shopkeeper lowers the awnings.

My body. In time. And the hour passes.

Like Animals

To give birth to ourselves each day makes this death
an act of will, and stopping here to say goodbye is all too sadly
      telling.
The air is limned with secrets, and we are painted tenderly,
and awkward. A breeze stirs up our alibis, but
they can be rewritten, and later still the fact of our desire.
It's enough to kiss the surface, a twitch
distinguished from afar, the regions
of our sufferings mapped out upon a sleeve.
Enough that nothing's missing, that the chapters
line up perfectly, how once revealed we
never stop reacting, how we
become the only character, looking
upward, tying a shoe.

Half Circle

Your body has recovered you.
Fog, or stars, a leaf of spring, the little
veins you're tracing, the world's
still healthy here.
And mother's well, though
you're her sister now.
The man who always loved you
thinks he's free. The woman
who loved your husband
wants your sympathy.
And lawyers come.
Accountants.
You can talk to them
at least, and do, the way
the city's here.

A rock's thrown
through the window.
A man's beaten in the hall.
The same young woman, night to night,
sleeps against your door.
The man who always loved you
thinks that you
belong to him. The woman
who loved your husband
counts you as a friend.
A new neighbor
phones. Bankers

call. Even the girl who
stole your purse tracks you down.
You can't accept, of course.
Her need is greater.

It Takes a While to Disappear

The city purrs, it hums along, the morning hardly risen.
A well-dressed drunk smears her finger across a doorman's lips and
        whispers.
Someone stumbles. Someone curses. Someone hoses down the
        pavement.
We must have made a mess of things again, all fuzzy black and white
and greenish at the corners. Some final thing
that put us in our places.

You're still standing in your winter coat alongside
everything you wanted and deserve. But you were thinner. The desk
        clerk
looked right through you. The cabby didn't listen. You were
out of sorts back then, you say, but
you're still frowning!

In vain a shrieking siren repeats itself
and fades. The quiet idles there, a crosswalk signal chirping. You're still
standing in your winter coat, but I don't know you. Someone
scrambles down a fire escape, his shirt a flag
that's shredded. A boy

salutes. And then his mother, too.
She stoops to smooth his collar. She makes a sculpture of her packages.
You're a different person now, you say, but
you will never happen.

Decalogue

Nothing hidden. Leaflessly grey
and cold. Only one car
below.

Nothing spared. A small boy
gently walking alone. His eyes are dark and wide-open
naturally. The pond is a short cut. Its thin ice

tested by his father hours ago.

———

Water dripping from the ceiling is the world to a man
in a coma. His wife stalks the doctor.
If he lives

she will abort the baby of her lover. He won't
and she cancels her appointment.
And he does.

———

There now.
7 a.m. in a station is not arbitrary.

You were not alone. And at one minute past

with your gloved fingers
you let it go.

———————

A letter arrives. It was written
twenty years ago. It never need be opened.
We found it

in a drawer because
we wanted to. Because we love and we are neither
parent nor child. We wished

for the impossible.
We did not know we were impossible.

———————

A young man accepts the cigarette.
He stubs it out. When
the trapdoor

opens
his hands twitch a little.
He could not

kill the cabby with a rope. He beat his face in
with a cudgel.
On the riverbank the quiet

took its time. He crushed that man
quickly with a stone.

A virgin answers all her questions.
He's in love. She's experienced. She instructs him.
They are not in her

apartment. Their
hands are not caressing. They are not excited
and do not suffer.

And oh how they've changed places.

Nearly every night. For a long time
a small girl screams and
screams.

She will not reveal her nightmare.
Again the light
comes early. On mountains of animals

she sleeps soundly.
And you are frightened too.

––––––––––

Nothing changes. It is spring. The man who
tried to save you cannot
speak.

The woman who sent you to your certain death
needs a friend. When
you pray

she prays.
Her husband turned away.
Back then the cups were of the finest china

but each was different. The oil lamp
unlit.

––––––––––

Lushly green
and cold. They'll adopt they say.
She will end it. And she does. He doesn't

know. She'll weep the way he
wept alone. Is it you
my love?

There?

———————

What you've achieved.
And other people's memories
of you.

You forget. It's childish
but nice.
Only money. Only

things. Your
kidney for a rose-colored stamp.
We're here

and nothing else exists.

Twilight

That he might just snap again was part of it, blind himself, and,
      well, you're there.
You'd climb the wooden stairs again, lock the bathroom door
      behind you, will yourself away.
                Maybe get it right this time, I don't know,
the card I thought to send, a thousand crows on a Chinese
      screen, a light from down below somewhere,
      everything.

Among schools of flashing fish, a shadow and its camera, we've
      all been there before.
Among the fruit and praying figures, his latest medication, his
      threatening, stupid call, each dangerous time.
You talk to him, put aside a little money for somebody else,
      pen messages, and stay. Move again.
                And it's a better story there,

it must be. The beginning of a street, a slant of houses. Glint
      and shimmerings, porches, and leaves. And now the
      twilight,
instantaneous. The tables, and the chairs. How the unseen
      break bread together, carefully.

Interior Landscape

In the blink of an eye, a light rain.
Among the ten-thousand synapses, the sound of rain, but
　　　delicately, the sound of leaves.

In the blink of an eye, a pure-cold air.
Were I swimming there, how clearly I could see my hands and
　　　everything they touch.

Among all shapes growing here and dying, a sweet
and earthy smell. The weight and feel spread thinly, my own
　　　blue house below,

as if the port were sighing, the cliffs
hauled in from afar, a wave of rolling tiled roofs and lamp stain
　　　splashed against the walls.

In the blink of an eye, no wonder.
In the blink of an eye, an empty room. The unread paper. The
　　　space I've cleared.

Alpine Wedding

All dark morning long the clouds are rising slowly up
beneath us, and we are fast asleep.
The mountains unmove

intensely. And so do we. Meadows
look down.

A city there looks up and
stirs a little. Adrift the rolling tiled roofs of
buildings, the deadly

trains of grinding sand and morning—
a spy unfolds his paper,

the coffee's served.

A bride and groom stand shivering on a tarmac
in the mist, and
they are happy. Each one

and all of us entangled, the room is moist with us,
the house unfinished, windowless,

and we are fast asleep.

The brother of the groom can't get
close enough. He leans against the brightest ridge
and ladder, the sucking

sound of memory
as heaven picks up speed and

hurtles through his burning skin
its frozen blankets
to the sun.

Between Murmur and Glare

Intense and
sudden brooding. Echoing. The ceiling
and the walls and the floor.

Between you and me
the furniture
gives ground. The hills

ease. Horizons
thin to the thin skies of the sea.
As a boat

to the window.
As anxious birds that seem always
to be starving.

On death. And
living. We can talk about living
between

islands.
On paper. Pure
glare. The strung lanterns

cutting into it.
Murmured on terraces. Laughter
in the square.

Like footsteps. Like tourists
streaming toward
evening.

Their shouts are words too.
Page after page of
dark water.

A Waltz for Debbie

As one swept swiftly past, and, lingering still, clings to but can't
      breathe the future. Or like the one who awakens as if
just falling off to sleep again, the dawn turns in its white robe,
      and looks back, and flies to the cold.

In the dream I know by heart, all is forgotten. Everything
      flares there. And is silent. In the shadow that knows
      me better, nothing's
changed, nothing doesn't change here. It's just a room, and the
      freed waters of the sea could talk me into anything.

And so the cliffs, and the wind, and their crowns of twigs are
      islands. A bright horizon, the mere
idea of you, so weirdly high upon the page.

The Vigil

Look again...the fence glistening in overcast light, the grass at
its brightest. Images of no one. Of one's own family,
burying itself. Rust-colored earth, or it seemed that
way—I don't remember.

Old fool, the mask is inside—no one sees through you but me.
And it's winter and pacing, the conversations you'll
have, and the person you speak to agrees.

But listen. Listen...how the living cry out in their cars, in the
stillness of sleep. The lover left out—pure harmony!

My love in the kitchen, paring apples—and why not? why
shouldn't she? The marvel of her hands, her head
tilted that way. Humming to herself, or dreaming,
smiling when she sees me—

what am I that your spirit's a killer!

And So Asks

Scissoring palm trees in the gorgeous light above.
Spires and gold-colored domes.
The blue of the avenue—
the air itself
handed down among crisscrossing
wires and rusted vanes

astonishes with our breathing
the pulse of shadows
and trains.

Blood blossoms the mortar—
newsprint and clutter and the chemical taste
the eye goes to
and savors,

and the stone too looks around.

From that which is not.
From that which is not but used to be and so asks
a stranger to snapshot our leaving—

that you were happy too,
relieved somehow and nicely tired,
and the smoke

and the hillsides drift by.

Tidy

I miss you too.
Something old is broken,

nobody's in hell.
Sometimes I kiss strangers,

sometimes no one speaks.
Today in fact

it's raining. I go out on the lawn.
It's such a tiny garden,

like a photo of a pool.
I am cold,

are you?
Sometimes we go dancing,

cars follow us back home.
Today the quiet

slams down
gently, like drizzled

lightning,
leafless trees.

It's all so tidy,
a fire in the living room,

a rug from Greece,
Persian rugs and pillows,

and in the kitchen,
the light

fogged with windows.

This

Today, my love,
leaves are thrashing the wind
just as pedestrians are erecting again the buildings of this drab
forbidding city,
and our lives, as I lose track of them,
are the lives of others derailing in time and
getting things done.
Impossible to make sense of any one face
or mouth, though
each distance
is clear, and you are miles
from here.
Let your pure
space crowd my heart,
that we might stay a while longer amid the flying
debris.
This moment,
I swear it,
isn't going anywhere.

From the Balcony

Out there, where whales swim upon a building and muffled
        harbor sounds collide. Where trains collide. A perfect
        slab of sea upon the specks of those who stroll upon
        its shore.

Among the very dawn of us, a single shrug of heart unleashes
        waves of birds and voices from the plaza. Then falls
        back again. And that much more denied.

One step of yours and cafés steam with coffee. A butcher parks
        outside our door. One nod and pots of blue
        chrysanthemum explode the blowing day.

Where echoes eat our papers. Real names, the fountains, rows
        of sycamore become their feathered haze. In our most
        human clothes, along the balustrades of all the gardens,

one breath is pure desire.

François Camoin

Ralph Angel is the author of three previous books of poetry: *Anxious Latitudes; Neither World,* which received the 1995 James Laughlin Award of The Academy of American Poets; and *Twice Removed.* He has also recently published a translation of Federico García Lorca's *Poem of the Deep Song.* His poems have appeared in scores of magazines and anthologies, both here and abroad, and recent literary awards include a gift from the Elgin Cox Trust, a Pushcart Prize, the 2003 Willis Barnstone Poetry Translation Prize, a Fulbright Foundation fellowship, and the Bess Hokin Award of the Modern Poetry Association. Mr. Angel is Edith R. White Distinguished Professor of English and Creative Writing at the University of Redlands, and a member of the MFA Program in Writing faculty at Vermont College. Originally from Seattle, he lives in Los Angeles.